Pebble™ Plus

Keeping Healthy

Taking Care of My Eyes

by Terri DeGezelle

Consulting Editor: Gail Saunders-Smith, PhD

Consultant: Amy Grimm, MPH
Program Director, National Center for Health Education
New York, New York

Capstone press

Mankato, Minnesota

Pebble Plus is published by Capstone Press,
151 Good Counsel Drive, P.O. Box 669, Mankato, Minnesota 56002.
www.capstonepub.com

 Books published by Capstone Press are manufactured with paper
containing at least 10 percent post-consumer waste.

Library of Congress Cataloging-in-Publication Data
DeGezelle, Terri, 1955–
    Taking care of my eyes / by Terri DeGezelle.
    p. cm.—(Pebble plus. Keeping healthy)
    Includes bibliographical references and index.
    ISBN-13: 978-0-7368-4260-0 (hardcover)
    ISBN-10: 0-7368-4260-8 (hardcover)
    ISBN-13: 978-1-4296-3824-1 (softcover)
    ISBN-10: 1-4296-3824-9 (softcover)
    1. Eye—Care and hygiene—Juvenile literature. I. Title. II. Series.
RE52.D44 2006
617.7—dc22   2004026745

Summary: Simple text and photographs present information on how to keep your eyes healthy.

Editorial Credits
Sarah L. Schuette, editor; Jennifer Bergstrom, designer; Stacy Foster, photo resource coordinator

Photo Credits
Capstone Press/Karon Dubke, all

The author dedicates this book to Sally DeGezelle.

Note to Parents and Teachers

The Keeping Healthy set supports science standards related to physical health and life
skills for personal health. This book describes and illustrates how to take care of your
eyes. The images support early readers in understanding the text. The repetition of words
and phrases helps early readers learn new words. This book also introduces early readers
to subject-specific vocabulary words, which are defined in the Glossary section. Early
readers may need assistance to read some words and to use the Table of Contents,
Glossary, Read More, Internet Sites, and Index sections of the book.

Printed in the United States of America in North Mankato, Minnesota.
012011
006069R

Table of Contents

My Amazing Eyes

My eyes help me see
the world around me.
My two eyes work together.

Pupils let light into my eyes.

Nerves inside my eyes

carry messages to my brain.

pupil

My brain understands

the messages.

Then I can see.

Checking My Eyes

I get my eyes checked
by an eye doctor.
I find out if I need glasses.

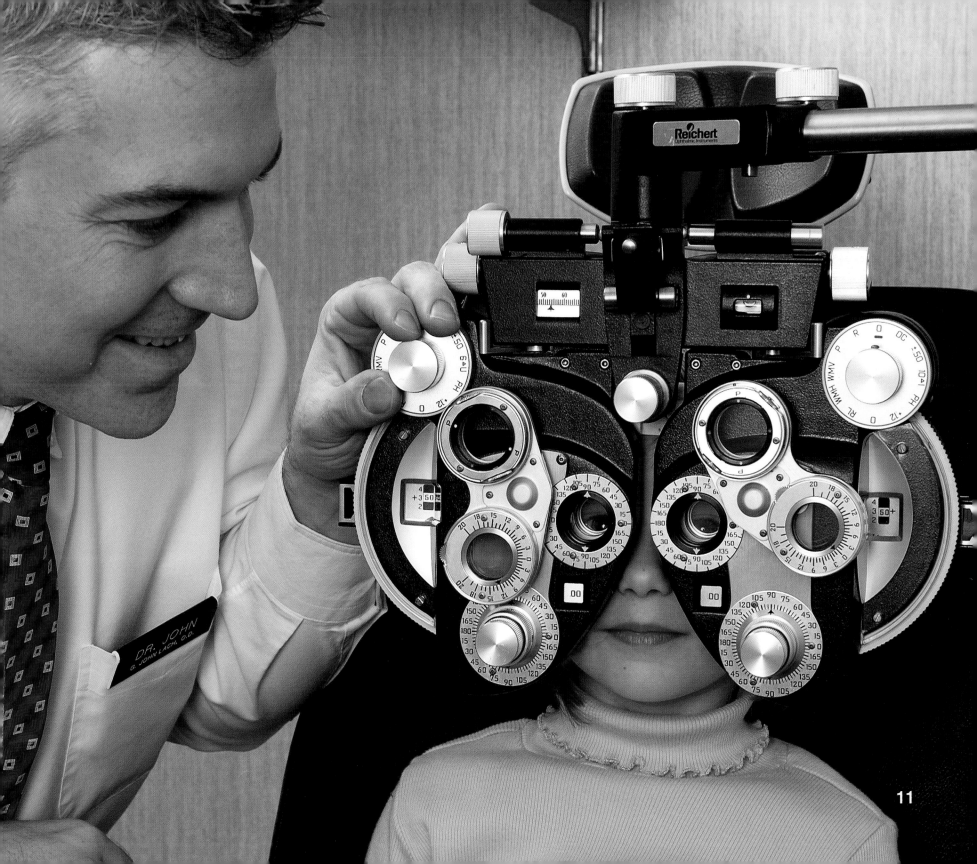

I go to the doctor

if my eyes are red and sore.

She tells me I have pinkeye.

She gives me medicine

to make it better.

Human Eye

Healthy Eyes

I keep my eyes healthy.

I make sure

there is enough light

when I read books.

The sun can hurt my eyes.

I wear sunglasses.

Looking at a computer screen

for a long time

can hurt my eyes.

I take breaks.

I stay healthy when

I take care of my eyes.

Glossary

brain—the body part inside your head that controls your body; your brain understands what your eyes see.

nerve—a bundle of thin fibers that sends messages between your brain and other parts of your body

pinkeye—a disease that makes eyes red, sore, and itchy; pinkeye can be spread from one person to another.

pupil—the round, dark center of your eye that lets in light

sight—the ability to see

Read More

Curry, Don L. *Take Care of Your Eyes.* Rookie Read-About Health. New York: Children's Press, 2005.

Llewellyn, Claire. *Seeing.* I Know That! North Mankato, Minn.: Sea to Sea, 2005.

Simon, Seymour. *Eyes and Ears.* New York: HarperCollins, 2003.

Internet Sites

FactHound offers a safe, fun way to find Internet sites related to this book. All of the sites on FactHound have been researched by our staff.

Here's how:

1. Visit *www.facthound.com*

2. Type in this special code **0736842608** for age-appropriate sites. Or enter a search word related to this book for a more general search.

3. Click on the **Fetch It** button.

FactHound will fetch the best sites for you!

Index

Word Count: 131
Grade: 1
Early-Intervention Level: 16